Copyright © Jonathan Lee 2004

Published by CWR, Waverley Abbey House, Waverley Lane, Farnham, Surrey GU9 8EP
The right of Jonathan Lee to be identified as the author and illustrator of this work has
been asserted by him in accordance with the Copyright, Designs and Patents Act 1988,
sections 77 and 78.

Bible verses taken from the Good News Bible © American Bible Society 1966, 1971,
1976, 1992, 1994.

See back of book for list of National Distributors.

Concept development, editing, design and production by CWR.

Illustrations: Jonathan Lee

Printed in England by Linney Print

ISBN: 1-85345-303-X

...Remember The Wise And Foolish Builders

Written and illustrated by Jonathan Lee

As another day came to a close the class gathered on the carpet to listen to Mrs Phips read from the Bible a parable Jesus taught. ... She cleared her throat, 'Uh hem', and began to read ...

This is a story about two men who wanted to build a house for themselves.

One was wise ...

...and the other was foolish.

The foolish man decided it would be easier for him to build his house on the soft sand. He quickly dug the foundations ...

... and piled on brick after brick.

It was all built in a flash. 'Phew', he said as he stood back to admire his work. He thought he had done well.

The wise man thought **differently**. He knew that sand could be easily moved but a **rock** was very secure.

By building his house on a rock he **took time** and care to make **sure** his house **would stand firm.**

Suddenly a great **storm** came with **lightning,** 'CRASH!' and waves

...ike tidal waves flooding in, 'SPLASH!' and a mighty wind, 'WHOOSH!'

The foolish man's house was completely destroyed.
Not one brick was left on top of another.

But the wise man's house stood firm and was not moved.
Just as he thought, the rock remained totally secure.

Jesus tells us that if we learn His teachings and obey them, we will be like the wise man that built his house on a rock.

Mrs Phips closed the Bible and asked the class if they had any questions.

Just then a boy called David put his hand up and asked, 'How can obeying what Jesus taught make us wise?'

'. . . remember to say **our prayers** . . .'

'. . . remember to be kind . . .'

'... remember to trust God ...'

'... remember to love one another.'

THE WISE AND FOOLISH BUILDERS

READ MATTHEW CH 7 v 24-28 AND HELP THE BUILDERS FILL IN THE [MISSING] WORDS

v24. 'So then, anyone who [____] these [____] of [____] and [____] them is like a [____] man who built his [____] on [____].'

v26. 'But anyone who [____] these words of [____] and [____] [____] [____] them is like a [____] man who built his [____] on [____].'

v25 '... it did ___ ___ ___, because it ___ ___ ___ on ___ ___ ;

v27 '... it ___ ___. And what a ___ ___ ___ that was;

MEMORY VERSE

Jesus says... 'If you love me, you will obey my commandments: (John Ch.14 v15)

COLOUR IN PAGES!!

Remember the Parables

In these first books of a brand new series, writer and illustrator, Jonathan Lee, presents well-loved parables in a unique blend of watercolour illustrations and text, which will delight children and adults alike. For children aged 3 to 6 years old.

36 pages

The Lost Sheep
ISBN: 1-85345-302-1

The Good Samaritan
ISBN: 1-85345-301-3

£ 3.99
Each (plus p&p)

National Distributors

UK: (and countries not listed below)
CWR, Waverley Abbey House, Waverley Lane, Farnham, Surrey GU9 8EP.
Tel: (01252) 784700 Outside UK (44) 1252 784700

AUSTRALIA: CMC Australasia, PO Box 519, Belmont, Victoria 3216.
Tel: (03) 5241 3288

CANADA: Cook Communications Ministries, PO Box 98, 55 Woodslee Avenue, Paris, Ontario.
Tel: 1800 263 2664

GHANA: Challenge Enterprises of Ghana, PO Box 5723, Accra.
Tel: (021) 222437/223249 Fax: (021) 226227

HONG KONG: Cross Communications Ltd, 1/F, 562A Nathan Road, Kowloon.
Tel: 2780 1188 Fax: 2770 6229

INDIA: Crystal Communications, 10-3-18/4/1, East Marredpally, Secunderabad – 500 026.
Tel/Fax: (040) 7732801

KENYA: Keswick Books and Gifts Ltd, PO Box 10242, Nairobi.
Tel: (02) 331692/226047 Fax: (02) 728557

MALAYSIA: Salvation Book Centre (M) Sdn Bhd, 23 Jalan SS 2/64,
47300 Petaling Jaya, Selangor.
Tel: (03) 78766411/78766797 Fax: (03) 78757066/78756360

NEW ZEALAND: CMC Australasia, PO Box 36015, Lower Hutt.
Tel: 0800 449 408 Fax: 0800 449 049

NIGERIA: FBFM, Helen Baugh House, 96 St Finbarr's College Road, Akoka, Lagos.
Tel: (01) 7747429/4700218/825775/827264

PHILIPPINES: OMF Literature Inc, 776 Boni Avenue, Mandaluyong City.
Tel: (02) 531 2183 Fax: (02) 531 1960

REPUBLIC OF IRELAND: Scripture Union, 40 Talbot Street, Dublin 1.
Tel: (01) 8363764

SINGAPORE: Armour Publishing Pte Ltd, Block 203A Henderson Road,
11–06 Henderson Industrial Park, Singapore 159546.
Tel: 6 276 9976 Fax: 6 276 7564

SOUTH AFRICA: Struik Christian Books, 80 MacKenzie Street,
PO Box 1144, Cape Town 8000.
Tel: (021) 462 4360 Fax: (021) 461 3612

SRI LANKA: Christombu Books, 27 Hospital Street, Colombo 1.
Tel: (01) 433142/328909

TANZANIA: CLC Christian Book Centre, PO Box 1384, Mkwepu Street, Dar es Salaam.
Tel/Fax (022) 2119439

USA: Cook Communications Ministries, PO Box 98, 55 Woodslee Avenue, Paris, Ontario, Canada.
Tel: 1800 263 2664

ZIMBABWE: Word of Life Books, Shop 4, Memorial Building,
35 S Machel Avenue, Harare.
Tel: (04) 781305 Fax: (04) 774739

For email addresses, visit the CWR website: www.cwr.org.uk

CWR is a registered charity – number 294387